EASY STUFFED VEGETABLES COOKBOOK

RECIPES FOR STUFFING EVERY TYPE OF VEGETABLE

By
Chef Maggie Chow
Copyright © by Saxonberg Associates

Published by
BookSumo, a division of Saxonberg Associates
http://www.booksumo.com/

INTRODUCTION

Welcome to *The Effortless Chef Series*! Thank you for taking the time to download the *Easy Stuffed Vegetables Cookbook*. Come take a journey with me into the delights of easy cooking. The point of this cookbook and all my cookbooks is to exemplify the effortless nature of cooking simply.

In this book we focus on Stuffed Vegetables. You will find that even though the recipes are simple, the taste of the dishes is quite amazing.

So will you join me in an adventure of simple cooking? If the answer is yes (and I hope it is) please consult the table of contents to find the dishes you are most interested in. Once you are ready jump right in and start cooking.

— Chef Maggie Chow

TABLE OF CONTENTS

Any Issues? Contact Me

If you find that something important to you is missing from this book please contact me at maggie@booksumo.com.

I will try my best to re-publish a revised copy taking your feedback into consideration and let you know when the book has been revised with you in mind.

:)

— Chef Maggie Chow

LEGAL NOTES

COMMON ABBREVIATIONS

cup(s)	C.
tablespoon	tbsp
teaspoon	tsp
ounce	oz.
pound	lb

*All units used are standard American measurements

Chapter 1: Easy Stuffed Vegetables Recipes

Decadent Stuffed Mushrooms

Ingredients

- 1 lb. mushroom
- 3 slices bacon, chopped fine, optional
- 1/2 C. chopped onion
- 1 clove garlic, finely chopped
- 1 C. shredded mozzarella cheese
- 1/2 C. soft breadcrumbs

Directions

- Set your oven to 375 degrees F before doing anything else and lightly grease a baking sheet.
- Remove the stems of the mushrooms then chop them finely.
- In a skillet, heat a little oil and sauté the bacon, mushroom stems, onion and garlic till the onion becomes tender.

- Drain all the fat and with a slotted spoon, transfer the bacon mixture into a bowl.
- Add the remaining ingredients and stir to combine.
- Stuff the mushroom caps with the bacon mixture.
- Arrange the mushroom caps onto the prepared baking sheet in a single layer.
- Cook everything in the oven for about 10 minutes.

Amount per serving: 1

Timing Information:

Preparation	20 mins
Total Time	30 mins

Nutritional Information:

Calories	18.3
Fat	1.0g
Cholesterol	2.9mg
Sodium	46.4mg
Carbohydrates	1.0g
Protein	1.2g

* Percent Daily Values are based on a 2,000 calorie diet.

STUFFED GARDEN VEGGIES

Ingredients

- 7 large mushrooms
- 4 tomatoes
- 3 zucchini
- 1 lb. ground pork

- 1 onion, diced
- 15 oz. diced tomatoes
- 1/2 C. mozzarella cheese

Directions

- Set your oven to 375 degrees F before doing anything else and lightly grease a baking sheet.
- Remove the stems of 4 mushrooms then chop them finely.
- Cut the tomatoes in half and remove the seeds.
- Cut the 2 zucchinis in half lengthwise and scoop out the pulp from the center.
- Sprinkle the vegetables with the salt and black pepper.
- Chop the remaining mushrooms and zucchini finely.
- Heat a nonstick skillet on medium heat and cook the ground pork, onion and seasoning till browned.

- Add the chopped mushrooms, mushroom stems and chopped zucchini and cook till tender.
- Stir in the tomatoes and cook for about 10 minutes.
- Stuff the vegetables with the pork mixture and sprinkle everything with the cheese.
- Place the vegetables onto the prepared baking sheet in a single layer and cook everything in the oven for about 35-45 minutes.

Amount per serving: 6

Timing Information:

| Preparation | 15 mins |
| Total Time | 1 hr |

Nutritional Information:

Calories	289.3
Fat	18.6g
Cholesterol	61.8mg
Sodium	270.4mg
Carbohydrates	13.9g
Protein	18.3g

* Percent Daily Values are based on a 2,000 calorie diet.

STUFFED BELL PEPPERS ITALIAN STYLE

Ingredients

- 6 green bell peppers

Beef Mixture:

- 1 lb. ground beef
- 1/2 C. onion, chopped
- 1 tbsp garlic, minced
- 1 egg, whisked
- 1/2 C. breadcrumbs
- 1 tbsp parmesan cheese
- 1 tsp salt
- 1 tsp ground pepper
- 1 tsp red pepper flakes (optional)
- 1/2 tsp oregano
- 1/4 tsp parsley

Quick Tomato Sauce Topping:

- 1 C. tomato sauce
- 1/4 C. water
- 1 tbsp brown sugar
- 1 tbsp vinegar
- 1 tsp prepared mustard
- 1 tsp Worcestershire sauce
- 1/4 tsp dried oregano
- 1/4 tsp dried basil
- 1/4 tsp garlic powder
- 1/4 tsp parsley flakes
- 1/4 tsp salt
- 1/4 tsp pepper

Directions

- Set your oven to 350 degrees F before doing anything else and lightly grease a baking dish.
- Cut off the tops of the bell peppers and discard the seeds from the inside.
- In a pan of boiling water, blanch the bell peppers for about 5 minutes.
- In a large bowl, add all the beef mixture ingredients and mix till well combined.
- In another bowl, mix together all the tomato sauce ingredients.
- In the bottom of the prepared baking dish, spread about 2 tbsp of the tomato sauce evenly.
- Stuff each bell pepper with the beef mixture evenly and top with the remaining tomato sauce.
- Place the vegetables over the tomato sauce in a single layer and cook everything in the oven for about 50-60 minutes.

Amount per serving: 4

Timing Information:

Preparation	10 mins
Total Time	1 hr 5 mins

Nutritional Information:

Calories	400.5
Fat	19.8g
Cholesterol	124.7mg
Sodium	1294.7mg
Carbohydrates	28.4g
Protein	27.8g

* Percent Daily Values are based on a 2,000 calorie diet.

Old-Fashioned Stuffed Cabbage Leaves

Ingredients

- 12 cabbage leaves
- 1 lb. ground beef
- 1 C. cooked rice
- 1 (15 oz.) can tomato sauce, divided
- 1 tsp garlic salt
- 1/4 tsp pepper
- 1/2 C. chopped onion
- 1/4 C. chopped green pepper
- 1 tsp sugar
- 1 tbsp cornstarch
- 1 tbsp water

Directions

- Set your oven to 350 degrees F before doing anything else.
- In a bowl, add beef, rice, green peppers, onion, garlic, 1/2 C. of tomato sauce, salt and black pepper and mix till well combined.
- Place about 1/3 C. of the beef mixture in each leaf and roll around the filling by tucking the sides.
- In another bowl, mix together sugar and the remaining tomato sauce.

- Arrange the cabbage rolls into a baking dish, seam-side down and top with the tomato sauce mixture evenly.
- Cook everything in the oven for about 45 minutes.
- Place the cabbage rolls on a plate and transfer the baking dish juices in a small pan.
- In a bowl, mix together the water and cornstarch.
- Add the cornstarch mixture in the pan and bring to a boil.
- Cook, stirring continuously for about 1 minute.
- Serve the cabbage rolls alongside the sauce.

Amount per serving: 4

Timing Information:

Preparation	10 mins
Total Time	55 mins

Nutritional Information:

Calories	371.6
Fat	17.4g
Cholesterol	77.1mg
Sodium	650.5mg
Carbohydrates	28.8g
Protein	24.9g

* Percent Daily Values are based on a 2,000 calorie diet.

THANKSGIVING STUFFED CELERY

Ingredients

- 1 bunch celery, separated
- 1 (8 oz.) packages cream cheese
- 2 tbsp sour cream
- 1/4 C. chopped walnuts
- 20 small green olives, chopped roughly

Directions

- You can remove the celery strings if you like.
- In a bowl, mix together the sour cream and cream cheese and fold in the olives and walnuts.
- Stuff the celery sticks with the olives mixture.
- Cut everything into the desired size pieces and refrigerate to chill before serving.

Amount per serving: 10

Timing Information:

| Preparation | 15 mins |
| Total Time | 15 mins |

Nutritional Information:

Calories	110.1
Fat	10.4g
Cholesterol	26.0mg
Sodium	106.8mg
Carbohydrates	2.5g
Protein	2.5g

* Percent Daily Values are based on a 2,000 calorie diet.

SUMMERTIME STUFFED ZUCCHINIS

Ingredients

- 7 fresh zucchini (4-6 inches long)
- 1/2 C. onion, chopped
- 1/4 C. olive oil
- 1/2 C. fresh mushrooms, coarsely chopped
- 1 garlic clove, minced
- 1 (3 oz.) packages cream cheese
- 1 egg, beaten
- 1/2 C. parmesan cheese
- 3/4 C. fresh parsley, chopped
- 1/8 tsp pepper
- parmesan cheese

Directions

- Set your oven to 350 degrees F before doing anything else.
- Cut the zucchinis in half lengthwise and with a spoon, scoop out the pulp, leaving about 1/4-inch inside, then chop the zucchini pulp finely.
- In a large skillet, heat the oil on medium heat and sauté the onion till tender.

- Stir in the chopped zucchini pulp, mushrooms and garlic and cook till all the liquid is absorbed.
- Stir in the Parmesan, cream cheese, egg, parsley and black pepper and cook for about 10 minutes.
- Remove everything from the heat and keep aside to cool slightly.
- Stuff the zucchini shells with the mixture evenly.
- Place the zucchini shells in a large jelly roll pan in a single layer and cook everything in the oven for about 30 minutes.

Amount per serving: 7

Timing Information:

Preparation	15 mins
Total Time	55 mins

Nutritional Information:

Calories	192.8
Fat	15.3g
Cholesterol	46.2mg
Sodium	178.6mg
Carbohydrates	8.7g
Protein	7.2g

* Percent Daily Values are based on a 2,000 calorie diet.

ORIENTAL STUFFED ACORN SQUASH

Ingredients

- 1 large acorn squash, halved and seeded
- 2 tbsp butter
- 2 tbsp onions, chopped
- 1/2 C. broccoli floret, chopped
- 1/4 C. mushroom, chopped
- 2 tbsp celery, chopped
- 2 tbsp walnuts, chopped
- 1/2 tsp brown sugar
- 1/2 tsp soy sauce
- 1 tbsp fresh basil, chopped
- 1/4 C. muenster cheese, grated

Directions

- Set your oven to 400 degrees F before doing anything else.
- Sprinkle the cut side of the acorn squash with the salt and black pepper.
- In a baking dish, place the acorn squash, cut-side down and cook everything in the oven for about 35 minutes.
- Meanwhile in a large skillet, melt the butter and sauté the onion till tender.

- Add the mushrooms, broccoli and celery and sauté for about 4 minutes.
- Stir in the basil and walnuts and remove everything from the heat.
- Top with the soy sauce, brown sugar and seasoning and toss to coat.
- Remove the acorn squash from the oven and stuff it with the veggie mixture.
- Sprinkle everything with the cheese evenly and cook everything in the oven for about 5 minutes.

Amount per serving: 2

Timing Information:

| Preparation | 10 mins |
| Total Time | 54 mins |

Nutritional Information:

Calories	304.7
Fat	20.8g
Cholesterol	44.0mg
Sodium	292.5mg
Carbohydrates	27.2g
Protein	7.4g

* Percent Daily Values are based on a 2,000 calorie diet.

Family Friendly Stuffed Bell Peppers

Ingredients

- 1 (14 1/2 oz.) can vegetable broth
- 1/4 C. water
- 1 bay leaf
- 1 C. quinoa
- 2 medium red peppers
- 2 medium yellow peppers
- 2 medium orange peppers
- 4 medium carrots, finely chopped
- 2 medium onions, finely chopped
- 1 tbsp canola oil
- 1 tbsp sunflower seeds
- 2 tsp parsley
- 1/2 tsp salt
- 1/2 tsp basil
- 1/2 tsp oregano
- 1/2 tsp paprika
- 1/8 tsp marjoram
- 1/8 tsp thyme
- 1 dash cayenne pepper
- 1 C. spaghetti sauce
- 1/4 C. parmesan cheese

Directions

- Set your oven to 350 degrees F before doing anything else and grease a 15x10-inch baking dish.
- In a pan, add the water, broth and bay leaf and bring to a boil.

- Stir in the quinoa and reduce the heat.
- Simmer everything for about for 15-20 minutes till all the liquid is absorbed.
- Remove everything from the heat and discard the bay leaf.
- Cut the bell peppers in half lengthwise and remove the seeds.
- In a large pan of boiling water, blanch the bell peppers for about 3-5 minutes.
- Drain and rinse under cold water.
- In a large skillet, heat the oil and sauté the onion and carrot till tender.
- Add the sunflower kernels, quinoa, herbs and seasoning and cook till heated completely.
- Stuff the bell pepper halves with the quinoa mixture and top everything with the spaghetti sauce and cheese.
- Arrange the bell pepper halves in the prepared baking dish and cook, covered in the oven for about 20-25 minutes.

Amount per serving: 6

Timing Information:

Preparation	30 mins
Total Time	1 hr

Nutritional Information:

Calories	211.4
Fat	5.3g
Cholesterol	0.0mg
Sodium	229.6mg
Carbohydrates	36.2g
Protein	6.7g

* Percent Daily Values are based on a 2,000 calorie diet.

Wonderful Shrimp Stuffed Eggplant

Ingredients

- 1 medium eggplant
- 1 medium onion
- 1 garlic clove
- 1/2 C. small raw shrimp
- 1/4 C. fresh basil, chopped
- 2 tbsp breadcrumbs
- salt and pepper
- 1/2 C. swiss cheese, shredded

Directions

- Set your oven to 350 degrees F before doing anything else and lightly, grease a baking dish.
- Cut each eggplant in half lengthwise and scoop out the pulp.
- In a shallow pan of boiling water, cook the eggplant shells till a little tender.
- Drain well.
- In a skillet, heat a little oil and sauté the onion and garlic till tender.
- Stir in the eggplant pulp and cook till done completely.
- Stir in the shrimp and cook for about 5 minutes.

- Add the basil, salt, black pepper and enough breadcrumbs till a firm mixture forms.
- Stuff the eggplant shells with the shrimp mixture.
- Arrange the eggplant shells in the prepared baking dish and cook everything in the oven till heated completely.
- Serve hot with a sprinkling of cheese.

Amount per serving: 2

Timing Information:

Preparation	30 mins
Total Time	1 hr

Nutritional Information:

Calories	147.3
Fat	1.3g
Cholesterol	0.0mg
Sodium	112.1mg
Carbohydrates	31.6g
Protein	5.5g

* Percent Daily Values are based on a 2,000 calorie diet.

STUFFED CUCUMBER BITES FOR SUMMER

Ingredients

- 1/4 C. crumbled blue cheese
- 1/2 C. cream cheese, softened
- 3 tbsp sour cream
- 1 tbsp minced green onion
- 1/2 C. chopped walnuts
- 2 cucumbers

Directions

- With a fork, score each cucumber longwise to create a striped effect.
- Slice the ends of each cucumbers then cut into 3/4-inch rounds.
- Scoop out the seeds from the center to create a shell.
- In a bowl, mix together the sour cream, cream cheese, blue cheese, green onion and walnuts, reserving about 1 tbsp.
- Stuff the cucumber shells with the cream mixture evenly and refrigerate to chill before serving.
- Serve with a garnishing of remaining walnuts.

Amount per serving: 1

Timing Information:

| Preparation | 15 mins |
| Total Time | 15 mins |

Nutritional Information:

Calories	44.1
Fat	3.9g
Cholesterol	7.1mg
Sodium	36.9mg
Carbohydrates	1.5g
Protein	1.1g

* Percent Daily Values are based on a 2,000 calorie diet.

AROMATIC STUFFED TOMATOES

Ingredients

- 5 beefsteak tomatoes
- 1 C. flat leaf parsley, chopped
- 3/4 C. Italian seasoned breadcrumbs
- 1 C. provolone cheese, grated
- 1/4 tsp ground black pepper
- 1 tsp butter, softened
- 2 tbsp extra virgin olive oil
- 1 garlic clove, finely minced

Directions

- Set your oven to 375 degrees F before doing anything else and grease a baking dish.Cut each tomato in half horizontally and separate the pulp.
- Chop the tomato pulp and transfer into a bowl.
- Add the remaining ingredients except oil and mix till well combined.
- Stuff the tomato shells with the herb mixture.

- Place the tomato shells in the prepared baking dish in a single layer and drizzle with the oil evenly.
- Cook everything in the oven for about 20 minutes.

Amount per serving: 6

Timing Information:

Preparation	20 mins
Total Time	50 mins

Nutritional Information:

Calories	202.3
Fat	12.1g
Cholesterol	17.0mg
Sodium	472.9mg
Carbohydrates	15.4g
Protein	8.9g

* Percent Daily Values are based on a 2,000 calorie diet.

THANKSGIVING STUFFED SQUASH

Ingredients

- 1 (2 -4 lb.) kabocha squash
- 1 tbsp butter
- 1 medium apple, diced
- 1/2 C. fresh cranberries, frozen can also be used
- 2 tbsp brown sugar
- 2 tbsp chopped pecans, toasted
- 1/2 tsp cinnamon

Directions

- Set your oven to 350 degrees F before doing anything else and grease a large baking dish.
- Cut the squash in half and scoop out the inner pulp.
- Arrange the squash in a prepared baking dish, cut-side down and cook everything in the oven for about 35 minutes.
- Meanwhile heat a skillet on medium heat and cook the butter, apple, cranberries, pecans, brown sugar and cinnamon till the butter melts.
- Reduce the heat to low and simmer till apple just become tender.

- Remove the squash from the oven and fill each half with the apple mixture.
- Again, cook everything in the oven for about 25-35 minutes.

Amount per serving: 2

Timing Information:

Preparation	5 mins
Total Time	1 hr 15 mins

Nutritional Information:

Calories	403.5
Fat	16.7g
Cholesterol	15.2mg
Sodium	65.7mg
Carbohydrates	67.2g
Protein	5.9g

* Percent Daily Values are based on a 2,000 calorie diet.

Stuffed Artichokes in Italian Style

Ingredients

- 4 medium fresh artichokes
- 2 -3 C. Italian style breadcrumbs
- 2 -3 tbsp of grated parmesan cheese
- 1 tbsp dried parsley
- 1 tsp garlic salt
- 1/2 tsp fresh ground black pepper
- 1/4 C. extra virgin olive oil
- 1 -2 tbsp extra virgin olive oil (for drizzling)

Directions

- Set your oven to 375 degrees F before doing anything else.
- Tug the leaves of the artichokes to loosen slightly and trim off the stems.
- Then remove the pointed tips of the leaf.
- In a large bowl, mix together all the ingredients except the olive oil.
- Slowly, add 1/4 C. of the oil, mixing continuously till well combined.
- Place the cheese mixture over each artichoke leaf, starting from the bottom.

- Arrange the artichokes in a baking dish and add about 1-inch of water.
- Drizzle the artichokes with the remaining oil and tightly cover with foil.
- Cook everything in the oven for about 60-80 minutes.

Amount per serving: 4

Timing Information:

Preparation	20 mins
Total Time	1 hr 20 mins

Nutritional Information:

Calories	437.8
Fat	20.6g
Cholesterol	2.2mg
Sodium	556.4mg
Carbohydrates	53.3g
Protein	12.6g

* Percent Daily Values are based on a 2,000 calorie diet.

Mexican Stuffed Eggs

Ingredients

- 6 hard-boiled eggs (cold, halved and yolks removed)
- 1 avocado, mashed
- 2 tbsp salsa, your favorite
- Garnish
- 12 cilantro leaves

Directions

- In a bowl, mix together the salsa and mashed avocado.
- Stuff each egg half with the salsa mixture.
- Serve immediately with a garnishing of cilantro.

Amount per serving: 12

Timing Information:

| Preparation | 10 mins |
| Total Time | 15 mins |

Nutritional Information:

Calories	66.2
Fat	5.1g
Cholesterol	93.2mg
Sodium	48.1mg
Carbohydrates	1.8g
Protein	3.5g

* Percent Daily Values are based on a 2,000 calorie diet.

Stuffed Tomatoes & Peppers in Greek Style

Ingredients

- 5 medium perfectly-ripe yummy tomatoes
- 5 medium green peppers
- 3/4 C. olive oil
- 13 tbsp rice
- 1 large onion, chopped fine
- 3 garlic cloves, minced very fine
- 1/4 C. fresh spearmint, minced
- 1/2 C. parsley, minced
- 1/2 C. pine nuts
- 1/2 C. parmesan cheese, cut into tiny cubes
- 1/2 C. raisin
- 1 tsp salt
- 1/2 tsp pepper
- 1 1/2 C. water
- 1/2 C. olive oil
- 1 tbsp tomato paste
- salt and pepper

Directions

- Set your oven to 375 degrees F before doing anything else.
- Cut the top of each pepper and discard the seeds and membrane.

- Cut the top of each tomato and scoop out the pulp, then chop it finely.
- Arrange the peppers and tomatoes in a large baking dish in a single layer and sprinkle with a little sugar.
- In a bowl, add the tomato pulp, onion, garlic, herbs, rice, cheese, raisins, salt, black pepper and 3/4 C. of the olive oil and mix till well combined.
- Stuff the peppers and tomatoes with the rice mixture.
- In a bowl, mix together the tomato paste, water, salt, black pepper and remaining oil.
- Place the oil mixture around the peppers and tomatoes.
- Cook everything in the oven for about 1 hour and 45 minutes.
- Turn off your oven but keep the baking dish in the oven for about 1 hour before serving.

Amount per serving: 8

Timing Information:

Preparation	1 hr
Total Time	2 hrs 45 mins

Nutritional Information:

Calories	496.0
Fat	40.0g
Cholesterol	0.0mg
Sodium	319.9mg
Carbohydrates	33.5g
Protein	4.6g

* Percent Daily Values are based on a 2,000 calorie diet.

STUFFED JALAPEÑOS IN ITALIAN STYLE

Ingredients

- 1 lb. bulk pork sausage
- 1 (8 oz.) packages cream cheese, softened
- 1 C. shredded parmesan cheese
- 22 large jalapeno peppers, halved lengthwise and seeded
- ranch dressing

Directions

- Set your oven to 425 degrees F before doing anything else and grease a 13x9-inch baking dish.
- Heat a large nonstick skillet on medium heat and cook the sausage till done.
- Drain the fat and transfer the sausage into a bowl.
- Add the parmesan, cream cheese and stir to combine well.
- Stuff each jalapeño half with the cheese mixture.
- Place the jalapeño halves in the prepared baking dish in a single layer and cook everything in the oven for about 15-20 minutes.
- Serve with ranch dressing.

Amount per serving: 1

Timing Information:

Preparation	20 mins
Total Time	40 mins

Nutritional Information:

Calories	60.0
Fat	4.5g
Cholesterol	17.3mg
Sodium	59.0mg
Carbohydrates	0.7g
Protein	3.8g

* Percent Daily Values are based on a 2,000 calorie diet.

REFRESHING STUFFED ENDIVE SPEARS

Ingredients

- 1/2 C. diced black olives
- 2 tbsp pine nuts
- 8 oz. cream cheese, softened
- 1/4 C. sun-dried tomato packed in oil, finely chopped
- 1/4 C. fresh basil, chopped
- 1 clove garlic, minced
- 1/4 tsp red pepper flakes, crushed
- 3 heads Belgian endive
- basil sprig (to garnish)

Directions

- In a large bowl, mix together the all ingredients except the endive and the basil sprigs.
- Trim the end of each endive head then separate everything into spears.
- Place the cheese mixture over the endive spears evenly.
- Serve immediately with a garnishing of basil.

Amount per serving: 1

Timing Information:

Preparation	15 mins
Total Time	15 mins

Nutritional Information:

Calories	37.4
Fat	2.6g
Cholesterol	4.9mg
Sodium	57.7mg
Carbohydrates	1.9g
Protein	2.0g

* Percent Daily Values are based on a 2,000 calorie diet.

STUFFED POTATOES CUBAN STYLE

Ingredients

- 1 lb. ground beef
- 4 baking potatoes
- 1 1/2 C. grated cheddar cheese
- 1/2 C. milk
- 2 tbsp mayonnaise

- 1 small onion, diced
- 1 dash garlic salt
- salt & pepper
- butter, cheddar cheese and sour cream

Directions

- Roast the potatoes till tender.
- Remove them from the oven and let them cool completely.
- Set your oven to 350 degrees F for baking the potato shells and grease the baking dish.
- Cut the potatoes in half lengthwise and scoop out the flesh.
- Heat a nonstick skillet and cook the beef with the salt and black pepper till browned.
- Drain the fat and transfer into a bowl.

- Add the potato flesh, and the remaining ingredients and stir to combine well.
- Stuff the potato shells with the beef mixture.
- Place the potato shells in the prepared baking dish in a single layer and cook everything in the oven for about 30 minutes.

Amount per serving: 4

Timing Information:

Preparation	35 mins
Total Time	35 mins

Nutritional Information:

Calories	588.2
Fat	34.7g
Cholesterol	127.7mg
Sodium	411.3mg
Carbohydrates	32.7g
Protein	35.4g

* Percent Daily Values are based on a 2,000 calorie diet.

Fabulous Stuffed Avocado

Ingredients

- 2/3 C. crumbled feta cheese
- 2 small ripe tomatoes, chopped
- 1/2 red onion, chopped
- 2 tbsp chopped fresh parsley
- 2 tbsp olive oil
- 1 tbsp red wine vinegar
- 1 tsp oregano
- 2 large avocados, halved and pitted

Directions

- In a large bowl, mix together all the ingredients except the avocado.
- Stuff the avocado halves with the feta mixture and serve everything immediately.

Amount per serving: 4

Timing Information:

Preparation	15 mins
Total Time	15 mins

Nutritional Information:

Calories	333.9
Fat	29.8g
Cholesterol	22.2mg
Sodium	291.9mg
Carbohydrates	14.5g
Protein	6.5g

* Percent Daily Values are based on a 2,000 calorie diet.

STUFFED EGGPLANT ITALIAN STYLE

Ingredients

- 2 small eggplants
- 1 tsp salt
- 3 tbsp oil
- 1 medium onion, diced
- 1 green pepper, diced
- 1 small zucchini, cubed
- 2 garlic cloves, diced
- 1 (6 oz.) cans tomato paste
- 1 tsp sugar
- 1/2 tsp salt
- 1/4 tsp black pepper
- 1 tsp oregano
- 2 C. cooked kidney beans
- 8 oz. muenster cheese, grated

Directions

- Cut each eggplant in half lengthwise and scoop out the flesh, leaving about 1-inch of shell.
- Chop the eggplant flesh and transfer into a bowl.
- In a pan, add 1/2-inch of the water and salt and place the eggplant shells, skin-side down.
- Bring to a boil on high heat, then reduce the heat to low and simmer everything for about 10 minutes.

- Drain well and keep aside.
- In a large skillet, heat the oil and sauté the reserved eggplant pulp, zucchini, bell pepper, onion and garlic till tender.
- Stir in the beans, sugar, tomato paste and seasoning and simmer everything for about 10 minutes.
- Stuff the eggplant shells with the vegetable mixture.
- Place the eggplant shells in the prepared baking dish in a single layer and cook everything in the oven for about 10 minutes.

Amount per serving: 4

Timing Information:

Preparation	20 mins
Total Time	1 hr

Nutritional Information:

Calories	536.4
Fat	28.9g
Cholesterol	54.5mg
Sodium	1956.3mg
Carbohydrates	49.4g
Protein	25.6g

* Percent Daily Values are based on a 2,000 calorie diet.

WONDERFULLY DELICIOUS STUFFED TOMATOES

Ingredients

- 1/2 C. breadcrumbs
- 1/2 C. parmesan cheese
- 3 tbsp parsley, chopped
- 2 tbsp chives, chopped
- 1 tsp tarragon
- 1 tsp pepper
- 1 small onion, finely chopped
- 4 medium-size tomatoes, ripe
- 4 oz. unsalted butter, melted

Directions

- Set your oven to 350 degrees F before doing anything else and grease a baking dish. In a bowl, mix together all the ingredients except the tomatoes. Cut a thin slice from the top of each tomato and scoop out the seeds.
- Stuff each tomato with the cheese mixture.
- Place the tomatoes in the prepared baking dish in a single layer and cook everything in the oven for about 10 minutes.

Amount per serving: 8

Timing Information:

| Preparation | 15 mins |
| Total Time | 25 mins |

Nutritional Information:

Calories	171.9
Fat	13.8g
Cholesterol	35.9mg
Sodium	150.9mg
Carbohydrates	8.7g
Protein	4.2g

* Percent Daily Values are based on a 2,000 calorie diet.

SCRUMPTIOUS STUFFED POTATOES

Ingredients

- 4 medium baking potatoes
- 1/4 C. butter
- 1/4-1/3 C. half-and-half cream
- salt and pepper
- 1 C. shredded cheddar cheese
- 1/4 C. finely chopped green onion
- 1 package imitation crabmeat, chopped

Directions

- Set your oven to 425 degrees F before doing anything else.
- Roast the potatoes for about 45-50 minutes. Remove from the oven and let them cool completely. Cut the potatoes in half lengthwise and scoop out the flesh. In a bowl, add the potato flesh, cream, butter, salt and black pepper and mas till smooth.
- Stir in the green onions and cheese.
- Gently, fold in crabmeat.
- Stuff the potato shells with the crabmeat mixture.
- Cook everything in the oven for about 15 minutes.

Amount per serving: 4

Timing Information:

| Preparation | 5 mins |
| Total Time | 2 hrs 5 mins |

Nutritional Information:

Calories	355.5
Fat	22.7g
Cholesterol	65.7mg
Sodium	269.7mg
Carbohydrates	28.8g
Protein	10.2g

* Percent Daily Values are based on a 2,000 calorie diet.

FRENCH STYLE STUFFED MUSHROOM

Ingredients

- 2 large portabella mushrooms (stem and gills removed)
- 1 (8 oz.) chicken breasts
- 6 garlic cloves, smashed
- 1/4 tsp garlic salt
- 1/2 C. mashed potatoes
- 3 tbsp milk
- 1 tsp butter
- 1 tbsp extra virgin olive oil
- 1 tbsp butter
- 3 tbsp celery, chopped fine
- 2 tbsp shallots, chopped fine
- 2 tbsp green peppers, chopped fine
- 1/2 tsp basil
- 1/2 tsp cajun seasoning
- 2 tbsp white wine
- paprika

Directions

- Set your oven to 325 degrees F before doing anything else and lightly, grease a baking dish.
- In a large pan of boiling water, add the garlic and place a steamer basket in it.

- Place the chicken and garlic salt in the steamer basket and cook, covered till done completely.
- Remove everything from the heat and keep aside to cool completely, then chop finely.
- In a pan of boiling water, cook the potatoes till tender and drain well.
- Peel the potatoes and transfer into a bowl with the milk and 1 tsp of the butter and mash completely.
- In a large skillet, heat 1 tbsp of the oil and the remaining butter and sauté the bell peppers, celery and shallot for about 2 minutes.
- Stir in the wine and cook for about 1 minute.
- Stir in the chicken, Creole seasoning, salt and black pepper and remove everything from the heat.
- Stir in the mashed potato mixture.
- Stuff the mushroom caps with the chicken mixture and arrange into the prepared baking dish.
- Cook everything in the oven for about 15 minutes.
- Serve immediately with a sprinkling of paprika.

Amount per serving: 2

Timing Information:

Preparation	45 mins
Total Time	1 hr

Nutritional Information:

Calories	438.7
Fat	26.3g
Cholesterol	97.1mg
Sodium	313.5mg
Carbohydrates	20.3g
Protein	28.5g

* Percent Daily Values are based on a 2,000 calorie diet.

FESTIVE STUFFED MUSHROOM

Ingredients

- 12 large mushrooms
- 1 lb. fresh spinach
- 2 slices bacon, diced
- 1 small onion, finely chopped
- 1/2 tsp marjoram
- 2 egg yolks
- breadcrumbs, as required
- salt & freshly ground black pepper
- 1/2 C. grated gruyere cheese

Directions

- Heat the broiler of your oven.
- Remove the stems of the mushrooms then chop the stems finely.
- In a large pan of boiling water, blanch the spinach for about 2 minutes.
- Drain well, then squeeze and chop it.
- Meanwhile, heat a nonstick skillet and cook the bacon till just cooked.
- Add the onion and sauté till just tender.
- Stir in the mushroom stems and cook for some minutes.

- Remove everything from the heat and stir in the spinach and marjoram.
- Add the egg yolks, salt, black pepper and the required amount of the breadcrumbs and mix till well combined.
- Stuff the mushroom caps with the spinach mixture and top with the cheese.
- Arrange the mushroom caps in a broiler pan and cook under broiler for about 10 minutes.

Amount per serving: 4

Timing Information:

Preparation	20 mins
Total Time	30 mins

Nutritional Information:

Calories	181.1
Fat	12.2g
Cholesterol	116.9mg
Sodium	237.2mg
Carbohydrates	8.6g
Protein	12.1g

* Percent Daily Values are based on a 2,000 calorie diet.

ITALIAN STUFFED OLIVES

Ingredients

- 1 can jumbo black olives
- garlic, cloves, as required
- olive oil, as required
- 1 tbsp italian seasoning
- 1 red chili pepper

Directions

- Drain the olives completely.
- Peel the garlic cloves and stuff each olive with a garlic clove.
- In a mason jar, add the olives, Italian seasoning, red chili and enough oil to cover the olives completely.
- Cover with a seal tightly and shake well to mix.
- Marinate everything for at least a few hours or ideally 1 day.

Amount per serving: 1

Timing Information:

Preparation	10 mins
Total Time	10 mins

Nutritional Information:

Calories	18.0
Fat	0.2g
Cholesterol	0.0mg
Sodium	4.0mg
Carbohydrates	3.9g
Protein	0.8g

* Percent Daily Values are based on a 2,000 calorie diet.

STUFFED ONIONS IN ITALIAN STYLE

Ingredients

- 4 medium onions
- olive oil flavored cooking spray
- 1 -2 tbsp butter, preferably unsalted
- 2 garlic cloves, finely minced
- 1 large potato, coarsely grated
- sea salt, to taste
- fresh ground pepper, to taste
- 1/2 tsp thyme
- mixed Italian herbs, to taste
- 1 tsp lemon juice
- 1 -2 C. baby spinach leaves, chopped
- 125 g freshly grated parmesan cheese
- 3 large eggs, lightly whipped
- 2 tbsp grated fresh parsley

Directions

- Set your oven to 400 degrees F before doing anything else and lightly, grease a baking dish.

- In a large pan of boiling water, cook the onions for about 15 minutes and drain well.
- Cut the onions in half and scoop out about 2/3 of the center.
- Chop the inner part of the onions finely.
- Arrange the outer onion rings on the prepared baking dish in a single layer.
- In a nonstick skillet, melt the butter and sauté the onion and garlic till tender.
- Stir in the grated potato and cook till the potato becomes crisp and tender.
- Stir in the baby spinach, thyme, salt, black pepper and lemon juice and remove everything from the heat.
- Immediately, stir in Parmesan and keep aside to cool slightly.
- Add the eggs and mix till well combined.
- Stuff the onion rings with the egg mixture and sprinkle everything with extra Parmesan.
- Cook everything in the oven for about 15 minutes.
- Serve with a garnishing of parsley.

Amount per serving: 6

Timing Information:

Preparation	10 mins
Total Time	50 mins

Nutritional Information:

Calories	225.0
Fat	10.5g
Cholesterol	129.1mg
Sodium	377.9mg
Carbohydrates	19.8g
Protein	13.3g

* Percent Daily Values are based on a 2,000 calorie diet.

Annie's Squash

Ingredients

- 4 pattypan squash (each about 3 inches in diameter)
- 4 tbsp butter
- 2 celery ribs, chopped
- 1/2 C. chopped onion
- 1/2 C. water
- 1 C. dry herb seasoned stuffing mix
- 4 oz. shredded sharp cheddar cheese

Directions

- Set your oven to 350 degrees F before doing anything else and grease an 8x8-inch baking dish.
- Cut the edges of each squash and discard the seeds.
- In a skillet, add the squash shells and about 1/4-inch of the water on high heat.
- Cover and bring to a boil then reduce the heat to medium-low.
- Simmer everything for about 5 minutes and drain.

- Place the squash shells in the prepared baking dish in a single layer and keep aside.
- In a large skillet, melt the butter on medium-high heat and sauté the celery and onion till tender.
- Stir in the stuffing mix and water and cook till all the liquid is absorbed.
- Stir in the cheese and remove everything from the heat.
- Stuff each squash shell with the cheese mixture and cook everything in the oven for about 20-30 minutes.
- Serve immediately.

Amount per serving: 4

Timing Information:

Preparation	20 mins
Total Time	50 mins

Nutritional Information:

Calories	227.2
Fat	20.9g
Cholesterol	60.3mg
Sodium	275.0mg
Carbohydrates	2.9g
Protein	7.5g

* Percent Daily Values are based on a 2,000 calorie diet.

Italian Style Banana Peppers

Ingredients

- 4 banana peppers
- 4 slices bacon, chopped
- 2 small chopped onions
- 1 tbsp minced garlic
- 1/4 C. grated mozzarella cheese
- 1/4 C. grated mature tasty cheese
- 2 tsp mixed Italian herbs
- 2 tsp oregano
- 1/2 tsp salt

Directions

- Set your grill to medium heat. Cut off the tops of the banana peppers and discard the seeds from inside.
- In a large skillet, heat the oil and sauté the bacon, onion, garlic, Italian herbs, oregano and salt till tender.
- Transfer the bacon mixture into a bowl and immediately, stir in both cheeses. Stuff the banana peppers with the cheese mixture evenly. Cover each pepper with the tops and wrap everything with foil. Cook everything on the grill for about 15 minutes.
- Carefully, change the side and cook for about 10 minutes more.

Amount per serving: 4

Timing Information:

Preparation	5 mins
Total Time	25 mins

Nutritional Information:

Calories	188.8
Fat	14.7g
Cholesterol	29.6mg
Sodium	582.0mg
Carbohydrates	7.2g
Protein	7.4g

* Percent Daily Values are based on a 2,000 calorie diet.

SOUTHWESTERN STUFFED TOMATILLOS

Ingredients

- 20 tomatillos
- 2/3 C. cheddar cheese, shredded
- 1/2 C. whole kernel corn
- 6 oz. cream cheese, softened
- 2 green onions, sliced (with tops)
- 1 tsp ground red chili pepper
- ground red chili pepper (for garnish)

Directions

- Cut a thin slice from the top of each tomatillo and scoop out the seeds.
- With a paper towel, carefully pat dry the inside of each tomatillo.
- In a bowl, mix together the corn, green onion, cheddar cheese, cream cheese and 1 tsp of chili powder.
- Stuff each tomatillo with the corn mixture evenly and sprinkle everything with the remaining chili powder.
- Refrigerate to chill before serving.

Amount per serving: 1

Timing Information:

Preparation	20 mins
Total Time	20 mins

Nutritional Information:

Calories	59.9
Fat	2.7g
Cholesterol	13.3mg
Sodium	63.7mg
Carbohydrates	3.2g
Protein	2.0g

* Percent Daily Values are based on a 2,000 calorie diet.

Aromatic Stuffed Snow Peas

Ingredients

- 48 snow peas
- 8 oz. cream cheese, at room temperature
- 1/4 C. fresh parsley, chopped
- 1/4 C. fresh dill, chopped
- 1 clove garlic, minced
- black pepper

Directions

- In a pan of salted boiling water, blanch the snow peas for about 30 seconds.
- Transfer the snow peas into a bowl of cold water, then drain well and keep aside to cool completely.
- With a sharp knife, split the snow peas along the curved side.
- In a bowl, add the remaining ingredients and mix till well combined.
- Stuff the snow peas with the herb mixture evenly and refrigerate to chill before serving.

Amount per serving: 1

Timing Information:

| Preparation | 1 hr 15 mins |
| Total Time | 1 hr 16 mins |

Nutritional Information:

Calories	18.1
Fat	1.6g
Cholesterol	5.2mg
Sodium	14.3mg
Carbohydrates	0.4g
Protein	0.4g

* Percent Daily Values are based on a 2,000 calorie diet.

Milanese Tomatoes

Ingredients

- 6 tomatoes, firm, washed, and at room temperature
- 2 tbsp olive oil
- 2 tbsp fresh parsley, chopped
- 1 tbsp scallion, chopped
- 1 garlic clove, chopped
- 1 C. dry breadcrumbs
- 6 tbsp swiss cheese, grated

Directions

- Set your oven to 325 degrees F before doing anything else and grease a baking dish.
- Cut a thin slice from the top of each tomato and scoop out the seeds.
- With a paper towel, dry the tomatoes.
- In a large skillet, heat the oil on and cook the breadcrumbs, garlic and parsley till heated completely.
- Stuff each tomato with the parsley mixture evenly and sprinkle everything with the cheese.

- Place the tomatoes in the prepared baking dish in a single layer and cook everything in the oven for about 45 minutes, coating with the oil occasionally.

Amount per serving: 6

Timing Information:

Preparation	30 mins
Total Time	1 hr 15 mins

Nutritional Information:

Calories	160.1
Fat	7.5g
Cholesterol	6.2mg
Sodium	151.9mg
Carbohydrates	18.4g
Protein	5.3g

* Percent Daily Values are based on a 2,000 calorie diet.

STUFFED CAULIFLOWER INDIAN STYLE

Ingredients

- 1 tbsp ground turmeric
- salt
- 3 lbs head cauliflower, core trimmed
- 2 tbsp chickpea flour
- 1 C. plain low-fat yogurt
- 2 tbsp ginger paste
- 2 tbsp garlic paste
- 2 tbsp vegetable oil
- 1/4 C. roasted cashews, coarsely chopped
- 1/3 C. green beans, finely chopped
- 1 small carrot, finely chopped
- 1/4 tsp garam masala
- 1/4 tsp ground cumin
- 1/8 tsp cayenne pepper
- 1/8 tsp ground fenugreek
- 1 C. cottage cheese
- 1/4 C. cheddar cheese, shredded
- 2 tbsp dried currants
- fresh ground pepper

Directions

- Set your oven to 425 degrees F before doing anything else.

- In a large pan of boiling water, cook the cauliflower with the turmeric and 1 tbsp of the salt for about 15 minutes.
- Drain well and let it cool completely.
- In a small nonstick frying pan, stir fry the chickpea flour for about 2 minutes then transfer into a bowl and keep aside to cool completely.
- Add the yogurt, garlic paste, ginger paste, 1 tsp of the oil and salt and mix till well combined.
- Add the cashews in a mini food processor and pulse till finely grounded.
- In a skillet, heat the remaining oil on low heat and cook the carrot and green beans for about 5 minutes.
- Stir in the spices and cook for about 1 minute more.
- Transfer the vegetables mixture into a bowl and keep aside to cool.
- Add the currants, both cheeses, ground cashews, salt and black pepper and stir to combine.
- Carefully, stuff the cauliflower head with the vegetable mixture in the crannies on the underside of the head and between the florets.
- Arrange the cauliflower head in a baking dish, right-side up and top with the yogurt mixture evenly.
- Cook everything in the oven for about 1 hour.

Amount per serving: 4

Timing Information:

| Preparation | 25 mins |
| Total Time | 1 hr 40 mins |

Nutritional Information:

Calories	359.8
Fat	17.7g
Cholesterol	20.0mg
Sodium	448.0mg
Carbohydrates	35.7g
Protein	20.2g

* Percent Daily Values are based on a 2,000 calorie diet.

Countryside Tomatoes

Ingredients

- 1 C. diced cooked carrot
- 1 C. cooked asparagus, sliced
- 1 C. cooked tiny peas
- 1/2 C. mayonnaise
- 1/2 C. sour cream
- 2 tbsp finely chopped onions
- 2 tsp lemon juice
- 1 tsp Worcestershire sauce
- 1 dash white pepper
- 8 medium tomatoes

Directions

- In a bowl, mix together the cooked vegetables.
- In another large bowl, add the remaining ingredients except the tomatoes and mix. Add the vegetables mixture and gently stir to combine well and refrigerate to chill for at least 1 hour.
- Cut a thin slice from the top of each tomato and scoop out the seeds, leaving about 1/2-inch shell. Sprinkle 8 C. with a little salt and invert tomatoes in each C. Refrigerate to chill before serving.
- Transfer the tomato shells on a plate and stuff each shell with the vegetables mixture evenly and serve.

Amount per serving: 8

Timing Information:

Preparation	5 mins
Total Time	5 mins

Nutritional Information:

Calories	77.9
Fat	3.2g
Cholesterol	7.4mg
Sodium	39.8mg
Carbohydrates	10.7g
Protein	3.0g

* Percent Daily Values are based on a 2,000 calorie diet.

STUFFED POBLANOS

Ingredients

- 3 tbsp olive oil, divided
- 1 large onion, diced
- 1 1/2 C. barley, soaked overnight and drained
- 1 bunch kale, thick stems removed, leaves chopped
- 1 1/8 tsp chili powder, divided
- 3 garlic cloves, minced
- 1 (28 oz.) can whole canned tomatoes, crushed
- 1/4 tsp kosher salt
- 6 large Poblano peppers
- 2 oz. low-fat white cheddar cheese, grated
- 2 oz. reduced-fat Monterey jack cheese, halved
- 1/2 C. crumbled queso fresco

Directions

- In a large pan, heat 1 tbsp of the oil on medium heat and sauté the onion for about 5-7 minutes.
- Stir in 3 3/4 C. of the water and barley and cook for about 30 minutes.

- Add the kale and about 1/8 tsp of the chili powder and cook till the kale is wilted.
- Stir in the cheddar cheese and remove everything from the heat.
- Meanwhile in another pan, heat the remaining oil on medium heat and sauté the garlic for about 3 minutes.
- Stir in the tomatoes, salt and the remaining chili powder and bring to a boil.
- Reduce the heat and simmer, stirring occasionally for about 30 minutes.
- Set your oven to broiler and arrange the rack in the middle position.
- Cut off the stems of the poblano peppers and reserve them.
- Carefully, remove the seeds and membrane.
- Stuff the poblano peppers with the barley mixture and cover with the reserved stems.
- Arrange the peppers in a broiler pan in a single layer.
- Cook the peppers under the broiler for about 20 minutes, flipping once half way.
- Now, remove the stems of the peppers and sprinkle everything with the Monterey Jack cheese evenly.
- Broil for about 1-2 minutes.
- Serve with a topping of the queso fresco evenly.

Amount per serving: 6

Timing Information:

Preparation	10 mins
Total Time	1 hr 5 mins

Nutritional Information:

Calories	349.2
Fat	10.6g
Cholesterol	1.9mg
Sodium	359.6mg
Carbohydrates	56.2g
Protein	13.0g

* Percent Daily Values are based on a 2,000 calorie diet.

RAW STUFFED AVOCADOS

Ingredients

- 2 C. kale, thinly sliced
- 1/4 tsp salt
- 1 lime, juice of
- 1 tbsp cold-pressed coconut oil
- 1 garlic clove, minced
- 1/2 C. pineapple, diced
- 1/4 C. red bell pepper, diced
- 2 tbsp cilantro, chopped
- 2 tbsp scallions, chopped
- 1/8 tsp chipotle pepper
- 2 avocados

Directions

- In a bowl, add the kale and salt and massage with your hands till wilted and soft.
- Add the garlic, coconut oil and lime juice and massage again.
- Add the remaining ingredients and toss to coat well.
- Cut the avocado in half lengthwise and remove the pit.
- Place the kale mixture into the avocado halves evenly and serve immediately.

Amount per serving: 4

Timing Information:

Preparation	10 mins
Total Time	10 mins

Nutritional Information:

Calories	227.3
Fat	18.4g
Cholesterol	0.0mg
Sodium	168.5mg
Carbohydrates	17.4g
Protein	3.5g

* Percent Daily Values are based on a 2,000 calorie diet.

Augustinian Peppers

Ingredients

- 3 large baking potatoes
- 3 large red peppers, halved and seeded
- 1 1/2 C. sour cream
- 7 oz. gouda cheese, shredded
- 1 bunch green onion, chopped
- 4 tbsp butter
- 3 tbsp parsley flakes
- 1/2 tsp salt
- 1/2 tsp ground black pepper
- 1/4 tsp seasoning salt
- 1/4 tsp paprika

Directions

- Set your oven to 450 degrees F before doing anything else.
- Roast the potatoes for about 1 hour.
- Meanwhile set your grill to heat.
- In a pan of boiling water, blanch the red bell pepper halves for about 5 minutes.
- Drain well and cool completely.

- Cut the roasted potatoes in half lengthwise and scoop out the flesh from inside then mash it.
- In a large bowl, add the potato flesh, butter, sour cream, cheese, green onion, parsley, seasoning salt, salt and black pepper and mix till well combined.
- Stuff the bell pepper halves with the cream mixture evenly and sprinkle everything with the paprika.
- Arrange the bell pepper halves in a foil pan and place the pan on the grill.
- Cover the grill with the lid and cook for about 15 minutes.

Amount per serving: 6

Timing Information:

Preparation	10 mins
Total Time	1 hr 10 mins

Nutritional Information:

Calories	396.7
Fat	28.5g
Cholesterol	88.0mg
Sodium	591.9mg
Carbohydrates	24.4g
Protein	12.3g

* Percent Daily Values are based on a 2,000 calorie diet.

STUFFED POTATOES MEXICAN STYLE

Ingredients

- 2 large baking potatoes, scrubbed
- 3 tbsp sour cream
- 3 tbsp table cream
- 1 C. cooked red kidney beans
- 1 C. mexicorn, cooked and drained
- 2 tbsp chopped cilantro
- salt and pepper
- 1/2 C. shredded extra-sharp cheddar cheese
- 1/2 C. salsa

Directions

- Roast the potatoes for about 40-60 minutes.
- Set your oven to 400 degrees F for baking the potato shells and grease a baking dish.
- Cut the roasted potatoes in half lengthwise and scoop out the flesh from inside.
- In a bowl, add the potato flesh, milk and sour cream and mash well.

- Add the corn, beans, cilantro, salt and black pepper and stir to combine.
- Stuff the potato shells with the bean mixture and sprinkle everything with the cheese.
- Arrange the potato shells in the prepared baking dish in a single layer and cook everything in the oven for about 20 minutes.
- Serve with a topping of salsa.

Amount per serving: 2

Timing Information:

| Preparation | 10 mins |
| Total Time | 1 hr 25 mins |

Nutritional Information:

Calories	556.7
Fat	20.1g
Cholesterol	58.8mg
Sodium	1018.4mg
Carbohydrates	76.7g
Protein	23.3g

* Percent Daily Values are based on a 2,000 calorie diet.

South-Western Stuffed Bell Peppers

Ingredients

- 4 medium red bell peppers
- 1/2 medium onion, chopped
- 2 C. frozen corn
- 2 (15 oz.) can black beans, drained and rinsed
- 2 tsp olive oil
- 1 tsp cumin
- 1 tsp cayenne pepper
- 1 garlic clove, minced
- 2 tsp cilantro, finely chopped
- 1 C. shredded cheddar cheese
- 1 C. shredded monterey jack pepper cheese

Directions

- Set your oven to 350 degrees F before doing anything else and grease a baking sheet.
- Cut the peppers in half lengthwise and remove the seeds.
- In a skillet, heat a little oil and sauté the onion till tender and transfer into a large bowl.
- Add the corn, black beans, garlic, cilantro, cayenne pepper, cumin and olive oil and mix well.

- Stuff the bell pepper halves with the beans mixture and top with both cheeses evenly.
- Arrange the bell pepper halves in the prepared baking sheet in a single layer and cook everything in the oven for about 8-10 minutes.

Amount per serving: 1

Timing Information:

Preparation	15 mins
Total Time	25 mins

Nutritional Information:

Calories	280.6
Fat	11.1g
Cholesterol	27.4mg
Sodium	168.7mg
Carbohydrates	31.6g
Protein	15.7g

* Percent Daily Values are based on a 2,000 calorie diet.

EASY STUFFED CABBAGE

Ingredients

- 8 large green cabbage leaves
- 1 lb. lean ground beef
- 1/4 C. chopped onion
- 2 tbsp chopped fresh parsley
- 3/4 tsp salt
- 1 tsp chopped fresh thyme
- 1 clove garlic, minced
- 1 pinch cayenne pepper
- 1 (8 oz.) can tomato sauce

Directions

- Set your oven to 375 degrees F before doing anything else and grease a baking dish.
- In a pan of boiling water, blanch the cabbage leaves for about 1 minute.
- Drain well and with a paper towel, pat dry the leaves completely.
- In a bowl, mix together the beef, onion, garlic, parsley, thyme, salt and cayenne pepper.
- Place the beef mixture over each cabbage leaf evenly.
- Fold each leaf around the filling and secure with toothpicks.

- Arrange the cabbage rolls in the prepared baking dish in a single layer, seam-side down and top with the tomato sauce.
- Cook everything in the oven for about 50-60 minutes.

Amount per serving: 4

Timing Information:

| Preparation | 20 mins |
| Total Time | 1 hr 20 mins |

Nutritional Information:

Calories	240.0
Fat	11.5g
Cholesterol	73.7mg
Sodium	823.7mg
Carbohydrates	9.3g
Protein	24.6g

* Percent Daily Values are based on a 2,000 calorie diet.

INCREDIBLE CHEESE STUFFED MUSHROOMS

Ingredients

- 7 large white mushrooms, stems removed
- 5 garlic cloves, crushed
- 3 -4 tbsp part-skim ricotta cheese
- 1/4 tsp salt
- 1/2 tsp cracked black pepper
- 1 tbsp olive oil
- 4 tbsp grated parmesan cheese

Directions

- Set your oven to 350 degrees F before doing anything else and grease a baking sheet.
- Chop 1 mushroom and the stems of the remaining mushrooms finely.
- In a skillet, heat the oil on medium heat and sauté the chopped mushroom and stems till just tender.
- Add the garlic, salt and black pepper and cook till done completely.
- Drain the fat and transfer the mixture into a bowl and let it cool slightly.

- Add the ricotta cheese and 2 tbsp of Parmesan and stir to combine.
- Stuff the mushroom caps with the cheese mixture and top with the remaining Parmesan.
- Arrange the mushroom caps in the prepared baking sheet in a single layer and cook everything in the oven for about 20-25 minutes.

Amount per serving: 2

Timing Information:

Preparation	10 mins
Total Time	30 mins

Nutritional Information:

Calories	164.3
Fat	11.7g
Cholesterol	15.8mg
Sodium	477.4mg
Carbohydrates	7.0g
Protein	9.4g

* Percent Daily Values are based on a 2,000 calorie diet.

Maggie's Favorite Mushrooms

Ingredients

- 2 (12 oz.) packages white button mushrooms
- 1 (8 oz.) packages cream cheese, softened
- 1 (8 oz.) packages sausage
- garlic, to taste
- 1/4 C. butter, melted

Directions

- Set your oven to 350 degrees F before doing anything else and grease a 13x9-inch baking dish.
- Chop the stems of the mushrooms finely.
- Heat a nonstick frying pan on medium-high heat and cook the sausage till just browned.
- Stir in the garlic and chopped mushroom stems and cook till done completely.
- Drain the fat and transfer the mixture into a bowl and let it cool slightly.
- Add the cream cheese and stir to combine.
- Place a little melted butter in the bottom of each mushroom cap.

- Stuff the mushroom caps with the sausage mixture and drizzle with the remaining melted butter.
- Arrange the mushroom caps in the prepared baking dish in a single layer and cook everything in the oven for about 30-45 minutes.

Amount per serving: 6

Timing Information:

Preparation	30 mins
Total Time	1 hr 10 mins

Nutritional Information:

Calories	343.2
Fat	31.8g
Cholesterol	83.9mg
Sodium	539.1mg
Carbohydrates	6.1g
Protein	10.3g

* Percent Daily Values are based on a 2,000 calorie diet.

THANKS FOR READING! NOW LET'S TRY SOME **SUSHI** AND **DUMP DINNERS**....

http://bit.ly/2443TFg

To grab this **box set** simply follow the link mentioned above, or tap the book cover.

This will take you to a page where you can simply enter your email address and a PDF version of the **box set** will be emailed to you.

I hope you are ready for some serious cooking!

http://bit.ly/2443TFg

You will also receive updates about all my new books when they are free.

Also don't forget to like and subscribe on the social networks. I love meeting my readers. Links to all my profiles are below so please click and connect :)

Facebook

Twitter

Come On...
Let's Be Friends :)

I adore my readers and love connecting with them socially. Please follow the links below so we can connect on Facebook, Twitter, and Google+.

Facebook

Twitter

I also have a blog that I regularly update for my readers so check it out below.

My Blog

CAN I ASK A FAVOUR?

If you found this book interesting, or have otherwise found any benefit in it. Then may I ask that you post a review of it on Amazon? Nothing excites me more than new reviews, especially reviews which suggest new topics for writing. I do read all reviews and I always factor feedback into my newer works.

So if you are willing to take ten minutes to write what you sincerely thought about this book then please visit our Amazon page and post your opinions.

Again thank you!

INTERESTED IN OTHER EASY COOKBOOKS?

Everything is easy! Check out my Amazon Author page for more great cookbooks:

For a complete listing of all my books please see my author page.

Printed in Great Britain
by Amazon

26253446R00071